CW01636137

GALE
CENGAGE Learning

Novels for Students, Volume 22

Project Editors: Sara Constantakis and Ira Mark Milne **Editorial**: Anne Marie Hacht

Rights Acquisition and Management: Sue Rudolph, Jessica Schultz, Timothy Sisler **Manufacturing**: Drew Kalasky

Imaging: Leitha Etheridge-Sims, Lezlie Light, Mike Logusz **Product Design**: Pamela A. E. Galbreath **Vendor Administration**: Civie Green

Product Manager: Meggin Condino

For more information, contact
Gale, an imprint of Cengage Learning
27500 Drake Rd.
Farmington Hills, MI 48331-3535
Or you can visit our Internet site at

ISBN 0-7876-6945-8
ISSN 1094-3552

Printed in the United States of America
10 9 8 7 6 5 4 3 2 1

The Woman in the Dunes

Kobo Abe

1962

Introduction

Kobo Abe, one of Japan's most celebrated and frequently translated authors and playwrights, is often compared to the Czech writer, Franz Kafka, because both writers created novels that were built upon nightmarish allegories. Abe's *The Woman in the Dunes* is a prime example. With this novel, one of Abe's more popular works, Abe takes the reader into a very strange and isolated world in order to make a statement about the condition of modern civilization. His statement is fascinating, but not very glorifying, as the protagonist becomes trapped in a world of ceaseless and mindless labor.

The Woman in the Dunes and the subsequent movie based on the novel catapulted Abe into the international realm. After the popular success of this novel, Abe's works became the most often translated fiction of Japanese literature. And long since its publication, *The Woman in the Dunes*, which in 1960 won the Yomiuri Prize for literature, continues to retain its classification of being not only the best of Abe's extensive life work, but also one of the classic examples of modern Japanese fiction.

The story begins with a character, Niki Jumpei, who seems all but totally unaware of who he really is. He often describes himself and his actions as if he were a detached observer of his own actions. His imprisonment in a hole in the sand dunes tempers his psyche, however, and in the end he comes to an awakening in which he grasps a better understanding of his basic psychological makeup. As Wimal Dissanayake, writing for *Literary Relations, East and West: Selected Essays* put it: "What Kobo Abe has sought to do is to remove his protagonist from his cultural environment and to probe deeper and deeper into his own psyche as a way of attaining his authentic selfhood." The story of a journey of inner discovery during which the protagonist remembers what it means to be human in a modern society that sometimes seems to have forgotten.

Author Biography

Kobo Abe, one of Japan's greatest writers, was born on March 7, 1924, in Tokyo. He followed in his father's footsteps to a certain extent, gaining a degree in medicine but quickly decided that he did not want to become a doctor. He much preferred storytelling. During his childhood, most of which was spent in the Manchurian city of Mukden, Abe entertained himself and his friends by reciting stories. Many of these tales came from the writings of Edgar Allan Poe; but Abe, even at an early age, created stories of his own. Having been raised outside of the main Japanese culture, Abe's writings and interests differed from those of many of his compatriots. He studied abstract painting instead of the traditional Japanese arts, and like his character in *The Woman in the Dunes*, Abe also studied insects.

Abe witnessed the atrocities and consequences of war, both in Mukden, and later, when he returned to Tokyo and read such Western writers as the German philosopher Martin Heidegger (1889–1976) and Czech novelist Franz Kafka (1883–1924) to find support for his own ideas against the militaristic Japanese government at that time, according to Raymond Lamont-Brown in his article in the *Contemporary Review*. But as Lamont-Brown states, "Abe's searches did not produce what he needed." When his father died, Abe felt released from his father's wishes that he become a doctor and decided to concentrate even harder on creating his own path. He dropped all efforts to pursue a medical profession and delved deeply into literature. If he could not find what he was looking for in the writings of others, he became determined to create what he was looking for on his own.

In 1951, Abe was awarded the Akutagawa literary prize for *The Crime of Mr. S. Karuma* and from this point, there was no turning back. His career was set, and his theme—that of alienation and loss of identity in modern society—was established and would be repeated throughout his life's work.

Some of Abe's most important novels include: *Suna no Onna* (1962) (*The Woman in the Dunes*, 1964); *Tanin no Kao* (1964) (*The Face of Another*, 1966); *Moetsukita Chizu* (1967) (*The Ruined Map*, 1969); *Hako Otoko* (1973) (*The Box Man*, 1975); and his last novel, *Kangaru Noto* (1991) (*The Kangaroo Notebook*, 1960).

Abe was also well known for his work in theater. He created his own drama group, which produced at least one of Abe's plays each year. He is remembered for such productions as *Tomodachi, Enemoto Takeaki* (1967) (*Friends*, 1969), and *Bo ni Natta Otoko* (1969) (*The Man Who Turned into a Stick*, 1975).

Abe married the artist Machi Yamada in 1947. The couple had one child, Neri. On January 22, 1993, Abe died, in Tokyo, of heart failure.

Plot Summary

Part 1

Kobo Abe's *The Woman in the Dunes* begins with a short summary of the main action of the novel. In this summary, the reader is told that a man has disappeared and since seven years have passed, he has been presumed dead. After this statement, the story flashes back to the day that this so-far unnamed man began what he thought would be a brief adventure to the seaside, in his search for an unusual insect. His hope is that he will find a bug that has yet to be classified. If he is the first to categorize it, his name will be attached to the insect's scientific classification. This will give the protagonist a sense of self identity.

Media Adaptations

- *The Woman in the Dunes* was adapted as a film in 1963, directed by Hiroshi Teshigahara and starring an all Japanese cast. The movie won the Jury Prize at Cannes in 1964. It was shot in black and white and can be viewed with subtitles. Image Entertainment recently converted the film to DVD format.

Upon arriving at the coast, the man discovers a village that is being all but buried by the drifting sand dunes. He does not pay much attention to the village, as he is focused on finding a particular beetle that he believes lives in the sand. As the sun sets, he is approached by one of the villagers, an old man, who asks if the protagonist is an inspector. Upon discovering that he is not, the old man asks where the protagonist plans to spend the night, as the last bus out of the village has already left. The protagonist suggests that he might stay at one of the villagers' houses, which the old man finally arranges.

The protagonist climbs down the steep slope of one of the sand dunes by way of a rope ladder and finds himself at the entrance of an old dilapidated house, which looks as if it could easily collapse under the weight of sand should a large enough amount blow onto it. Once on the sandy floor, a thirty-something-year-old woman greets him. She is not unpleasant to look at, he confesses, but he is a little disturbed by the rundown condition of her house and wonders if he is being taken as a fool. The woman feeds him dinner, but when he asks to take a bath, she informs him of her lack of water. He will have to wait until the day after tomorrow, she says. The protagonist laughs at this, telling her that he will be gone by then.

There are a series of brief discussions between the man and woman in which the man thinks the woman ignorant because she makes statements that are counter to his beliefs. One such comment that the woman makes is that the sand is damp, which the man refutes but later realizes how wet sand can be. Slowly, the man's reality begins to change as he sees things differently than he had previously. As the night progresses, he becomes nervous, sensing some inherent danger in his situation. A shovel and two buckets are dropped down into the pit where the house stands, for example, and a suggestion is made that the man should help the woman with her nightly chores, which consist of digging out all the sand that has fallen into the pit during the day. By the next morning, the man is on the verge of panic when he discovers that the rope ladder is nowhere to be found. It has been taken away. He tries to calm his nerves, cautiously asking the woman questions in an attempt to discover if she has indeed planned his entrapment. As all clues point to this sadistic conclusion, the man plans his escape. He will dig at the base of the sand dune, forcing the sand to slowly move toward the house, thus easing the angle of the slope. Or so he thinks. His knowledge of sand is faulty, once again, and he is all but buried in the sand when he starts digging as the slope collapses on him, and he passes out.

Part 2

The protagonist wakes up to the sounds of the woman cooking. He has been put to bed in the woman's house, and she is caring for him. He is feigning his injuries, though, falsely believing that if he does not work, the woman will not be able to do all the work and take care of him too, and the captors will see how useless the man is and will let him go. He tests his captors' willingness to cope with him by requesting a newspaper. He also hopes to find a story about himself as a missing person in the newspaper. There is no such story when the newspaper arrives, and the man is disappointed. He asks the woman why she allows herself to be used as a slave and tries to tempt her into demanding her freedom. But the woman is content with her life. The man thinks back on his life, wondering why no one has reported him missing. He describes the lives of those who were once around him and talks about Mobius man, with whom he tries to have a conversation about his inner thoughts. He also refers to the "other" woman, a woman with whom he had some kind of relationship. It is not clear if this is his girlfriend or a prostitute.

When the villagers seem to pay little mind to the fact that the man does not work, the protagonist grabs the woman and ties her up, forcing her to join him in not working. The villagers do pay attention to this but not in the way the man had hoped. Instead of releasing him as he demands, they quit bringing them water. The man asks the woman if the villagers have ever kidnapped and enslaved other outsiders. The woman tells him about a postcard dealer who was also entrapped. That man eventually died. There was also a young student. But no one has ever escaped, the woman tells him. The man begins to strip the wood of the house to make a ladder. He will not give up hope of finding a way out. When he threatens to take down the main supports of the house, the woman, whom the man has by now untied, tackles him to stop him. As they wrestle, they both become sexually aroused but do not act on it. The man flashes back to other sexual encounters with the other woman. He thinks about a venereal disease that he once had and wonders if the other woman gave it to him. A little later, the man and woman do have a sexual encounter. The next day, the man gives in and begs for water. They must work, the woman tells him, before the villagers will bring water. The man talks to the old man who brings the water and tries to convince him that he must let him go. The protagonist still believes he has the upper hand in the situation. He believes he can con his way out. But the old man does not give in. And once again, the protagonist refers to the fact that he thinks he is being taken advantage of, being laughed at. It has not completely dawned on him, however, that this is the exact truth.

There are hints in the next passages that the man is not disliking his situation as much as he had originally. He begins to like the ordinary things of his life in the sand dunes, the shoveling of the sand, the routine, and the nearness of the woman. But he does not stop planning his escape. He finally succeeds in creating a rope, and one day, as the woman sleeps, he climbs to the top of the roof, throws the rope to the top of the dune, where it anchors onto a sand bag, and climbs out of the hole. A fog hides him until nightfall, when he fumbles in the dark, trying to find his way out of the village. Unfortunately, he falls into a bog and sinks into it up to his waist and must be rescued. The villagers than take him back to the hole.

Part 3

A couple of months have passed. The man has set a trap for crows. If he catches one, he will wrap a note around its leg and hope that someone, other than the villagers, will read it and rescue him. The trap does not work. But one day, he finds that water has collected in the bottom of the trap. This excites him. He realizes that the villagers can never threaten him again by not bringing water to him. However, he becomes very stir crazy and craves seeing a different view, if only for a few minutes. He pleads with a group of villagers to let him out for just a few minutes. They say they might consider this if he first lets them watch as the man and woman make love. The protagonist agrees to this but the woman fights him off.

Time passes, and it is spring, and the woman is pregnant. One night she begins to bleed and must be taken away. In their hurry, the villagers forget to take away the rope ladder that they used to lift her out. The protagonist sees this, but he decides there is no hurry, and he does not escape.

Characters

Niki Jumpei

The protagonist Niki Jumpei has such an undeveloped sense of self that throughout most of the novel that he is not even given a name, but rather referred to only through the pronoun *he*. In the first lines of the story, the reader is told that the protagonist has disappeared. And at the end of the story, legal papers are offered to the reader in which Jumpei has been declared dead. The remainder of the story takes Jumpei through a challenge in which he must first shed his normal way of looking at life, and at himself, in order to find new definitions. He is placed in circumstances that are stark and confining, minimizing the details of his life down to the bare essentials. Jumpei fights his rebirth as he insists on hanging onto the old information that he has gathered so far in his life. He is rather haughty, looking down on those around him. Because of this, he stands apart from everyone and feels alienated. He constantly misjudges circumstances and people who filter in and out of his life. He is blind to what is happening to him because he refuses to take things at face value. By becoming so completely absorbed in trying to second-guess everyone, he completely misses the cues they offer him. This concentration on others causes him to also fail to understand himself. Not until Jumpei has failed miserably at everything he attempts does he finally realize that what he was looking for outside of himself is actually found within.

Mobius Man

A Mobius strip is a slip of paper that has been twisted once and then taped together to create a form that has no beginning and no end. Jumpei has given this name to a colleague of his, a man to whom Jumpei comes the closest to opening his more inner thoughts. Mobius Man listens without ridiculing Jumpei. The men discuss their philosophies of life. Jumpei thinks about Mobius Man often while he is in captivity. He does not have many discussions with the woman and so Jumpei turns to his thoughts of Mobius Man when he has a need for a deeper conversation.

Old Man

The old man is the only person who is singled out among the people of the village at the sea. It is the old man who first talks to Jumpei at the sand dunes, asking him how he is going to get back to town since the last bus has already left. It is also the old man who negotiates Jumpei's subsequent capture. The old man returns to the hole in which Jumpei is held prisoner. It is to the old man that Jumpei pleads to be released. The old man listens to Jumpei's requests but never changes his mind. In the old man's world, he needs Jumpei to remain exactly where he is, for the sake of the community.

Woman

The woman who lives in the sand dune is never given a name. At first, as seen through the eyes of the protagonist, she comes across as very innocent and somewhat backward. She easily submits to the horrid living conditions she must deal with in which she accomplishes back-breaking labor each day and a gritty existence at all other times. She flirts with Jumpei quite easily but it is not certain that she is doing this to entice him to stay or if it is just her childlike behavior, having had little contact with the outside word. But as the story progresses, the woman comes across more strongly. Shc fights back when Jumpei tries to rape her in front of the villagers, for instance. And she wrestles with Jumpei when he threatens to bring down the house. She is grateful for his presence, however, and is tender with him. She nurtures him, washes him, and tends to him when he is sick or hurt. In the end, her submissiveness teaches Jumpei to adapt to his surroundings, to enjoy the simplicity and the routine of the confining environment, and to see himself as he truly is.

Themes

Alienation

One of the overall themes in Abe's *The Woman in the Dunes* is that of alienation. The protagonist feels out of step with his society and is eventually cast into a situation that exemplifies his feelings. He is tossed into a hole and held captive in an environment that consists, for the most part, of only sand—a substance in which little if anything will grow. His surroundings consist of drab colors, stale air, and a lack of water. He remains totally dependent on outsiders to keep him alive. His attitude toward the woman with whom he shares a house is abrupt at best, but for most of the time it is caustic. He cannot relate to her acceptance of her dull life. While he is held captive, he recounts incidents from his former life as a schoolteacher. Although he is anxious for his freedom, his recollections of what his life was like outside the hole in the sand are not much more pleasant. He does not relate to his fellow teachers. He had been in some kind of relationship with a woman but it is unclear whether that relationship was as a lover and friend or if it were a relationship with a prostitute. Either way, the comments he makes about the "other" woman do not indicate that he enjoyed it. She always disagrees with him, he says, no matter what he tries to discuss with her. He is alienated from everyone, it seems, even from himself. He often refers to himself in an objective manner as if he were talking about someone else.

Loss of Identity

At the start of the novel, the protagonist searches for insects not so much to learn about them in any scientific way but rather so he might find an insect that has not yet been named. If he is successful, his name will be forever attached to the description of this bug. This will give him a sense of identity. As the readers find out later, the protagonist's identity is very much in question. As the story develops, it becomes obvious that he is not only looking for insects to immortalize his name, he is also looking for a true sense of himself. He has no identity, readers learn, other than insurance papers, birth certificate, and other pieces of paper that have his name on them. When he thinks of reasons why it is wrong for him to be held captive, he does not state the obvious, but rather he says that he is "someone who had paid his taxes, who was employed, and whose family records were in order." He is so lacking in a concept of himself that he often laughs without knowing why he is laughing. He senses pain but only as if that pain belonged to someone else. And when he cries, it is described in this way: "He sobbed in a stifled voice. But he was not particularly sad. He felt quite as if someone else were crying." But it is not only his emotions that he does not claim. There are moments when his body does not even seem to belong to him. For instance, at one point, as he goes to light a cigarette he is holding, and as he looks at his hand, he states: “The fingers that held it trembled.” A later section reads: “He felt that the hand he held to his face was floating free in the air.” This was his own hand he was talking about. Even in his description of having sex, it is said: “It was not he who had satisfied his desires, but apparently someone quite different, someone who had borrowed his body.”

Topics for Further Study

- Since Abe is often compared to Franz Kafka, read Kafka’s *Metamorphosis* and compare this with Abe’s *The Woman in the Dunes*. Both of these works are allegories. What does each work represent? How do they differ from one another? How are they the same? How do the endings differ?
- Critics often refer to Abe’s novel as

being affected by the philosophy of existentialism. Research this mode of thought and define what existentialism is. Who were some of the most influential thinkers of this philosophy? What writers infused their work with existential thought? Then explain how Abe's novel explores this philosophy.

- Read Yasunari Kawabata's *Snow Country*, which was written before the war. Focus on the way Kawabata describes the female characters in this novel. How do they compare to the way that Abe describes his female characters? Then pay attention to the male protagonist's emotions in Kawabata's novel and compare them to those of Jumpei in *The Woman in the Dunes*. Does Kawabata's protagonist discover something new about himself at the end? Which of the stories is more uplifting? And why?

- There have been great changes in Japan's long history. Choose three different time periods and compare the literature, the economy, and the culture. How did they change? What were the influences that caused these changes? How were these changes reflected in the literature of the times?

And in case these concepts of a lack of self were not clear enough, the protagonist mentions a mirror that is hung in the house in the sand pit. The paint on the back of the mirror has chipped away, and when anyone looks into it, they see only disjointed parts of themselves. And when the woman mentions that she wants to buy a new mirror, the protagonists says a new mirror would be just as useless. "What use would a mirror be to someone who no longer could be seen?" This loss of oneself builds up in the novel until the very last section. In the last pages, after he realizes that the sand contains drinkable water, the narrator states: "The change in the sand corresponded to a change in himself. Perhaps, along with the water in the sand, he had found a new self." And thus, the ending of the story is a new beginning, one in which the protagonist begins to create a true image of himself.

Impotency

The protagonist fights to retain some kind of power throughout most of the story. He threatens his captors, but his threats are weak and have no effect. He tries to escape several times but his plans are thwarted by the sand. He tries to catch a crow in his trap, but the crow is too smart to fall for it. Only at the end of the story, when he discovers water in his crow trap does the protagonist finally taste success. It is an accidental success, but the thought of it fills him with joy. He finally has something that works in his favor. He has water, the basis of life. It is at this point, when the feeling of impotency is finally lifted from his shoulders, that he finds a purpose and meaning to life.

Submission

The woman who lives in the sand dunes represents, in many ways, submission. She does not totally lack a will, but she often submits to her circumstances. She does not question why she cannot leave her house. She believes her endless digging of the sand is done in the name of the community. Whereas the man has lost his identity in the shuffling of paperwork in the modern society, the woman has acquiesced her identity in the name of her fellow villagers. She does what she is told. She lives according to the rules set upon her by others. She seldom talks back to the man even though what he says is often wrong. When he demands that she stop working, she obeys him. When he feigns illness and injury, she waits on him. When he talks about escaping, she ignores him.

Through most of the story, the man, on the other hand, fights against his circumstances. He constantly looks for an escape. It is not until the end of the story that he begins to understand the other side of submission. In the end it did not matter that he was stuck in a hole. After a failed escape attempt, the narrator recalls: “He was still in the hole, but it seemed as if he were already outside." The protagonist begins to realize that he had been lost in the details of life, much like a viewer might be lost in a mosaic by trying to see it by standing too close to it. In his new revelations, he felt as if "perhaps the world had been turned upside down and its projections and depressions reversed." What he once saw as submission, in other words, he now saw as tranquility.

Misunderstanding

As much as the protagonist believes he knows about life, the environment, and the people around him, he is constantly off the mark. This begins with his statement, at the beginning of the novel, that sand is dry. He later learns, to the contrary, that sand, in fact, is very wet. It is so wet that he can extract water from it. But this is not the only concept that is mixed up inside his head. He also believes, in the first section of the story, that the woman's submissiveness is wrong. "In every way that position [of submission] of hers was exceedingly dangerous." And once again, he is proven wrong. By the end of the story, it is the protagonist's submission that brings him peace. Again and again, the protagonist misjudges situations. He asks for a newspaper and expects to find an article about himself, but there is no such story. He threatens his captors by telling them: "You're going to be the ones in trouble if we're buried by the sand." Of course, this is ridiculous. He will be the one who is buried, and the villagers will find someone else to dig the sand. And when the villagers do not respond to him, the protagonist tells himself that “he was the one who held the fuse to the time bomb.” He says this as if he truly believes he is the one with the power. His concepts of reality and psychology are almost always wrong. He often thinks the woman is backwards or stupid such as when she tells him that the sand rots the wood. And when he tries to wrestle the shovel out of her hands, a task which he believes will be a simple one, he is caught off guard by her strength.

Style

Irony

The construction of *The Woman in the Dunes* includes many instances of irony. The overall ironic structure of the novel is that of the tables being turned on the protagonist. He hunts down and traps bugs for a hobby. And then he becomes like a bug, trapped in a hole in the sand. "He was lured on by the feeling that in all probability his prey was there, and he made his way down the gentle slope," the narrator relates in the beginning of the story. There are also many other examples of irony, most of them on a much smaller scale. A little later, the protagonist states that he was in "no special hurry," as he makes his way through the dunes before his capture. This is ironic because as soon as he realizes he is trapped, time weighs down on him almost to the point of his breaking. Then a few lines later, the protagonist sums up the village people with the words: "With their sense of caution appeased, they were merely good, simple fisherfolk." He will soon learn the irony of his own words. These people were neither simple nor merely good. Once he is lowered into the woman's house, the protagonist looks around himself and sees what a dilapidated condition the house is in, and the narrator states: "He would have thought they were making a fool of him and would doubtless have gone back at once." This is ironic on two fronts. First, they were making a fool of him and second, there was no way he could have gone back even if he had realized how foolish he was. At a later point, he misjudges the woman's actions, then he corrects his interpretation, stating to himself that "he certainly wouldn't be taken in again." Of course, at this point, he still does not have any realization that he already has been taken. And so Abe creates one ironic statement after the other. The reader knows what is going on and can laugh at the protagonist's continual naïveté.

Foreshadowing

Abe also uses foreshadowing, allowing the reader to sense what is coming as well as to create a dramatic sense of foreboding. Examples of foreshadowing include some of the protagonist's ironic thoughts before he is captured. For instance, there is the statement he makes as he wanders through the sand dunes, searching for insects. He says, at one point, "There was really nothing yet that foretold danger." In using this statement, Abe implants the sense of danger in the reader's mind even if it was not yet in the protagonist's thoughts. Then a few sentences later, Abe has the man thinking: "What in heaven's name could it be like to live there? he thought in amazement, peering down into one of the holes." Again, this is a mix of irony and foreshadowing. The protagonist's question, although he does not yet realize it, will soon be answered. He will be given a first-hand experience of what it is like to live in a hole in the sand. Yet later, as he continues to wander through the sand dunes, the protagonist concludes that the dunes represent “a disturbing and unsettling landscape.” He has no idea, at that point, how true his feelings are. And when he contemplates a fly, he makes an interesting statement about the insect’s adaptability. “The fact that the fly showed great adaptability meant that it could be at home even in unfavorable environments in which other insects could not live —for example, a desert where all other living things perished.” Much like the fly, the protagonist will also have to learn to adapt and to live in a hole in the sand.

Continuing his hunt for insects, the protagonist comments on the tactics of an entomologist, who “must concentrate his whole attention within a radius of about three yards around his feet.” In a short time, that will be almost all the space that he will have, as the narrow space of the house in the hole will be all that is granted to him. And finally, just before he is captured, he makes the observation: “No matter what they did, he mused, there was no escaping the law of the sand.” That law, the constant motion of the sand, and the inability to climb a steep cliff of sand, will also entrap him.

Scientific Details

Abe fills a lot of his narrative with scientific details. It is through these details that the protagonist seems to hold onto his sanity. His reality is filled with details. Most of these details, he has left behind in his former life. But the scientific ones have come with him and provide him with hope as he attempts to plan his escape. The scientific details also provide him with a mental stimulus that his rather barren surroundings do not allow. These details begin early in the story as he discusses the beetles that he has found and the ones he hopes to find. He talks about their body structure and their scientific names. He includes descriptions of the different types of vegetation he finds in the sand. And later, he makes the woman describe a bug she has seen. He asks several questions of her until he can name that particular beetle. But one of the major scientific discussions involves sand. The reader learns how sand is formed, what it is made of, how big its dimensions, how it drifts, *etc.* The protagonist later tries to create a theory of sand in order to imagine a particular construction of a house that might drift or float upon the sand, rather than be buried by it. He thinks in a scientific manner when he tries to scale the cliff of sand, digging at the bottom of the bank, calculating the angles of how the sand will fall and how much he will have to dig in order to make the cliff scalable. And then there are the scientific calculations that he uses to try and trap the crows, and his subsequent discovery of the capillary action of the sand in collecting water.

Allegory

The Woman in the Dunes is an allegory, a story that is symbolic of a specific point that the author is trying to make. The story serves as a way of expressing meanings other than those that first appear on the surface. The plot, setting, and characters merely represent abstractions that are the main focus of the author. In other words, the author wants the reader to feel or intuit what is actually behind these surface elements. Parables, many found in the Bible, and fables, as in children's stories, are allegories. Abe uses the forever-shifting sand, the entrapment, and the senseless and monotonous nightly labor of trying to save the woman's house as an allegory for the way he feels about the industrialized modern society and humankind's loss of meaning, self-worth, and identity.

Historical Context

Japan Immediately after World War II

On April 28, 1952, the official occupation of Japan by the United States ended. This did not, however, end the American influence on Japan, as Japanese officials had signed an agreement with the United States that established American military bases in the country. This agreement stated that the United States would protect Japan against any military attack by another country. The presence of the military, other government officials, as well as American businessmen, created an ever-widening change on the lives of the people of Japan. From clothes to music, from food to department stores, the ancient culture was rapidly becoming westernized. Japan was ruled by a new constitution; the emperor became more of a figurehead than a leader; and the country, in which most of its major cities had been destroyed, relied on American aid to get back on its economic feet.

Compare & Contrast

- **1960s:** Tokyo is considered to have experienced an economic miracle as it emerges from wartorn status, the results of World War II, to become

the second-largest economy in the world.
Today: Although the economic bubble that Tokyo enjoyed in the mid-twentieth century has burst, Tokyo remains one of the most modern and most thriving cities of all the industrial countries.

- **1960s:** Japanese literature in translation is studied in many U.S. universities, but the main focus of research is on ancient poetry, Noh drama, and classical literature such as *The Tale of Genji*, written in the eleventh century.
  Today: Japanese literature is considered one of the main components in the study of comparative literature as taught in U.S. universities. Modern Japanese novels, including those written by Japanese women, are now considered important topics of research.
- **1960s:** In 1968, Yasunari Kawabata becomes the first Japanese to win the Nobel Prize for literature.
  Today: Japan now has two Nobel Prize winners in literature, as Kenzaburo Oe joins Kawabata in winning the prize for his life's work.
- **1960s:** Japanese literature, which

had previously been described in terms of its beautiful aesthetics and multiple references to female beauty and nature, takes up new themes of alienation, loss of identity, loss of purpose, and the sense of defeat.

Today: The popularity of manga (Japanese comic books) has some critics worried that the younger Japanese generations will grow up without reading the more traditional forms of literature like novels and poetry.

For many years, despite the fact that Japan was now a democracy, only one party ruled the country. This allowed a certain stability in the region; and with the foreign aid they received, the Japanese people worked hard and were rewarded with one of the strongest economies in the world. Rapid rebuilding of its industries, which had almost been completely destroyed during World War II, was helped by the military needs during the United States involvement in the war with Korea in the 1950s. By the 1960s, Japan's economy had been quickly turned around.

Japan's Literature after World War II

Many Japanese authors were affected with

feelings of loss and alienation after their country's defeat and subsequent occupation after World War II. Some of the more influential writers of the 1940s, 1950s, and 1960s included Osamu Dazai, whose pessimistic views and characters often contemplated suicide because they could not cope with the changes they must face. One of Dazai's most remembered novels is *Ningen Shikkaku*, 1948, which was translated and published as *No Longer Human* in 1958. After many failed attempts, Dazai committed suicide in 1948.

Another great writer of that time period was Yuko Mishima, author of *Gogo No Eiko* (1963), translated the same year as *The Sailor who Fell from Grace with the Sea*. Mishima often wrote about suicide also, and performed seppuku, or ritualized suicide with a sword, in a much publicized event in 1970.

After the war, Nobel Prize–winning Kenzaburo Oe often wrote about rootless young people, such as in his most influential novel, *Kojinteki Na Taiken* (*A Personal Matter*), 1964. This story was influenced by the birth of his son, who was born with a congenital abnormality of the skull. In real life, doctors had suggested that Oe and his wife allow the child to die. Oe refused. Today, his son, Hikari, is a famous music composer. The birth of his son changed Oe's life and influenced his writing. He began to write against the use of nuclear weapons.

Japanese Educational System

Education is very important in Japan. The country enjoys high literacy rates, and a majority of high school students continue on to college. Although it has changed recently, during the post-War time period, getting into a secondary school in Japan was almost as difficult and challenging as it is today for a student in the United States to be accepted into college.

Although a form of education was present as early as the sixth century, the Japanese educational system was changed during the occupation by American forces. Education became compulsory until age sixteen, and schools were classified similar to the American system with elementary, middle, and secondary schools. Subjects taught are also similar to the school system in the United States, except that languages, especially English, are emphasized. Entrance exams are required in order to enter the last two years of secondary schools. And if a student does well on the exam and studies hard, he or she is all but guaranteed entrance into a well-respected college. The exams are tough, however, and schools specializing in studying for these exams are well attended. A popular term applied to this time of intense study is "examination hell." But almost half of all secondary students will eventually pass the exam and go on to college. Entrance exams into college, especially the more popular colleges, are also very difficult. But the rewards of gaining a degree from one of the more elite colleges is so profitable that prospective students will study for another year and retake the exam if he or she fails it the first time. Pressure to pass these exams begins as early as elementary school, during which time young students attend night classes to cram for the entrance exams they will one day have to take. This pressure has often been blamed for the emotional stress that many of Japan's children experience. This stress has been blamed for a rise in violence in school and in cases of suicide.

Critical Overview

The Woman in the Dunes remains a classic novel of Japanese literature almost half a century after it was published. As Myrna Oliver, writing for the *Los Angeles Times* put it, this first novel of Abe's "was considered a contender for the Nobel Prize for literature, but was not nominated, partly because the very private Abe studiously avoided the literary spotlight." Oliver continues her article by quoting Hisaaki Yamanouchi, who states one reason for Abe's popularity with Western readers: "Hc [Abe] is probably the first Japanese writer whose works, having no distinctly Japanese qualities, are of interest to the Western audience because of their universal relevance."

The Woman in the Dunes has been a popular favorite all over the world, sometimes bringing readers to their first experience of Japanese literature in translation. Abe's works, in general, are more easily translated because of their lack of allusions to traditional Japanese themes. *The Woman in the Dunes* focuses instead on problems that people all over the globe must face. Oliver continues her article on Abe by describing the protagonist, Niki Jumpei, as a man who "is first obsessed with the loss of his identity and with escape, but comes to realize that his sand prison gives him intellectual and spiritual freedom."

When *The Woman in the Dunes* was made into

a movie, Brent Kliewer, of the *Santa Fe New Mexican* offered these comments. He wrote that it "is a haunting allegory probing the fundamental questions of existence and the meaning of freedom." Kliewer continued by stating: "Its in the man's surrender to his circumstances that captured the imagination of the existential thinkers of the 60s." Existentialists believe that life is purposeless, a point that is at the heart of the novel.

One other critic, Kevin Thomas of the *Los Angeles Times*, who also viewed the movie, commented: "The late Kobo Abe provided Teshigahara [the director of the movie] with a metaphor for the human condition endlessly rich in implications." In one more review of the movie version, William Arnold, for the *Seattle Post-Intelligencer* wrote that, although the story can be enjoyed just on a surface level, if taken deeper, it provides "an existential allegory" and works "as an unforgettable and almost perfect metaphor for man's plight in a hostile world, and a lesson in how the individual must find his own meaning—and limits—in what is, in the end, a futile existence." Another movie critic, Jay Carr of the *Boston Globe* refers to the story as one on a level with Albert Camus's *The Myth of Sisyphus*. Carr then adds: "It's one of the great postwar statements of existential isolation, on a par with Beckett, Camus, Sartre."

From *The Washington Post* comes an article written by Anthony Thwaite, who calls *The Woman in the Dunes* "a hypnotic story of a struggle for existence." Thwaite continues by stating that the novel is "full of hard-edged detail and circumstantial stuff, at the same time it's a sort of parable about losing an identity and perhaps finding a new one." And finally, Wimal Dissanayake adds: "*The Woman in the Dunes* deals with the themes of alienation and identity, themes which are explored with the power of a fabulist imagination." And a little later in his article, Dissanayake continues: "*The Woman in the Dunes* communicates powerfully the emergence of the protagonist's newer self." Dissanayake points out that the focus of the novel is on the relationship between self and place and "Kobo Abe has explored this with a great measure of sensitivity and concreteness. His powerful visual imagination has caught this interplay with subtlety and cogency."

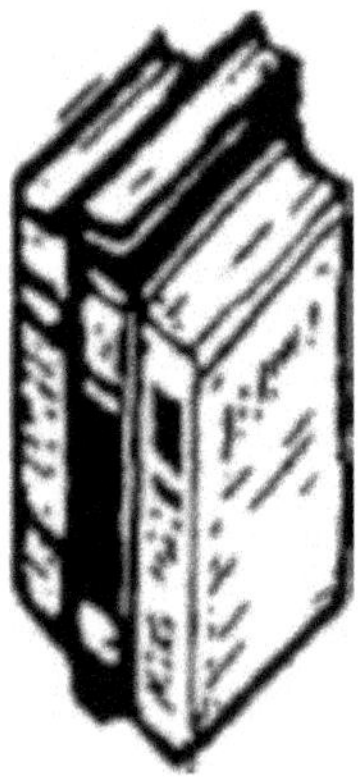

What Do I Read Next?

- Abe's *The Box Man*, published in 1975 in English, tells the story of an unnamed protagonist who goes around the city wearing a box over his head and constantly describing the world through his scribblings inside the box. This is a fable-like story of the loss of identity, its wonders, and its worries.

- In his novel *Ruined Map* (first published in English in 1969), Abe creates a mystery of a missing person. Mr. Nemuro disappeared more than six months ago, and his wife finally hires a detective to find him. The reader follows the detective in his search as Abe delves into the psychology of this man.
- *The Wind-Up Bird Chronicle* (1998), by Haruki Murakami, is a fascinating journey as the reader follows the protagonist in search of his wife and his cat who have gone missing. There is a lot of comedy mixed in with the morbidity of some of its characters, which include a prostitute, an ex-soldier, and a nasty politician.
- Yasunari Kawabata's *Snow Country* (first published in English in 1957) is about wasted love. It stands in stark contrast to Abe's style, giving the reader a deeper understanding of how revolutionary Abe's style was.

- Kenzaburo Oe's *A Personal Matter* (1964) relates the tension and concern of a father as he deals with a son whose brain is damaged at birth. This is considered Oe's best writing. The protagonist leads a rather shiftless life until he must face the responsibilities of fatherhood.
- Franz Kafka's *The Metamorphosis* (1915) is a nightmarish tale of a young man who awakens one morning to discover the horrific fact that he has been turned into a beetle-like bug. Kafka's effect on Abe was significant, and this story might shed some light on that influence.
- *Geisha: The Life, the Voices, the Art* (1995), by Jodi Cobb, provides an interesting look into the history of this ancient tradition in Japan. Cobb details everything from the intricate hair styles and makeup requirements to the intense training in the arts that these young women undergo. She also provides information on how demanding this profession can be despite the large amounts of money that the women are capable of making. This will provide the reader with a contrasted view of Japanese women that Abe only hints at.

Sources

Abe, Kobo, *The Woman in the Dunes*, Vintage International, 1991.

Arnold, William, "Years Enhance Eerie Feeling of Landmark Japanese Film *Woman in Dunes*," in *Seattle Post-Intelligencer*, January 23, 1998, p. 22.

Carr, Jay, "*Dunes*: An Allegory of Human Endeavor," in the *Boston Globe*, December 5, 1997.

Dissanayake, Wimal, "Self, Place, and Body in *The Woman in the Dunes*: A Comparative Study of the Novel and the Film," in *Literary Relations, East and West: Selected Essays*, edited by Jean Toyama and Nobuko Ochner, University of Hawaii Press, 1990, pp. 41–54.

Kliewer, Brent, "An Absurd View of Humanity," in *Santa Fe New Mexican*, December 19, 1997.

Lamont-Brown, Raymond, "Kobo Abe: Japan's Novelist of Alienation," in *Contemporary Review*, Vol. 263, No. 1530, July 1993, pp. 31–33.

Oliver, Myrna, "Kobo Abe, 68; Japanese Novelist and Playwright," in *Los Angeles Times*, January 23, 1993, p. 22.

Thomas, Kevin, "*Woman in the Dunes* an Erotic Masterpiece," in *Los Angeles Times*, September 5, 1997, p. 8.

Thwaite, Anthony, "Kobo Abe's Fables of Identity," in the *Washington Post*, April 21, 1991, sec. X, p. 6.

Further Reading

Henshall, Kenneth G., *A History of Japan: From Stone Age to Superpower*, Palgrave MacMillan, 2001.

> Through a study of politics, culture, literature, and economics, as well as other topics, Henshall provides a very spirited study of the history of Japan. Equal time is spent on both the classic periods as well as the modern.

Iles, Timothy, *Abe Kobo: An Exploration of His Prose, Drama, and Theatre*, European Press Academic Publishing, 2002.

> This is a critical study of Abe's life's work, including the influences that affected his writing.

Keene, Donald, *Five Modern Japanese Novelists*, Columbia University Press, 2003.

> Donald Keene is one of the most respected translators of Japanese literature. In this book, he examines the work of Kobo Abe, Junichiro Tanizaki, Yasunari Kawabata, Yukio Mishima, and Ryotaro Shiba—five of the best Japanese authors of the past century.

Murray, Giles, *Breaking into Japanese Literature*,

Kodansha International, 2003.

Giles Murray, an editor and writer living in Japan, has compiled a study of Japanese literature in both the original language and in translation. For students of Japanese, this is a great study tool. For others, it is a good way to sample some of Japan's best writing.

Shields, Nancy, *Fake Fish: The Theater of Kobo Abe*, Weatherhill, 1996.

Shields presents both a personal and a professional view of Kobo Abe's art as a playwright and director. This book is filled with anecdotes about Abe as well as a behind-the-curtain view of what it was like to work with Abe.

Varley, H. Paul, *Japanese Culture*, University of Hawaii Press, 2000.

From the effects of Zen Buddhism and the samurais to the modern influences of literature and comics, this is a comprehensive overview of what it might feel like to be brought up Japanese.

www.ingramcontent.com/pod-product-compliance
Ingram Content Group UK Ltd.
Pitfield, Milton Keynes, MK11 3LW, UK
UKHW020705240225
4725UKWH00043B/609

9 781375 394451